# AI Mirroring HI
## *Human Intelligence and Mindsets*

AI Mirroring HI
*Human Intelligence and Mindsets*

AI Mirroring HI

*Human Intelligence and Mindsets*

# AI Mirroring HI

Artificial Intelligence reflects

Human Intelligence and Mindsets

Dr. Farzana Chohan

AI Mirroring HI

*Human Intelligence and Mindsets*

AI Mirroring HI

*Human Intelligence and Mindsets*

Copyright © 2025 by Farzana Chohan

ISBN: 978-1-987931-21-1

# Dedication

**The Futuristic Human Mindsets!**

Your creativity and passion light the way towards a brighter world future. Especially our young folks, may your dreams and aspirations drive the innovations that will shape a peaceful and inclusive world. This book is dedicated to you, and to the promise of AI as a supportive ally in your journey, empowering you to achieve greatness and make a positive impact on the world.

# Table of Contents

# Introduction

The dawn of the 21st century has ushered in an era defined by the inexorable rise of Artificial Intelligence (AI). Once relegated to the realm of science fiction, AI has permeated our daily lives, from the algorithms that curate our social media feeds to the sophisticated systems driving autonomous vehicles. But beyond the practical applications, a profound question persists: can machines truly think, learn, and reason like humans? This book delves into the heart of this inquiry, exploring the intricate concept of "AI mirroring human intelligence," a pursuit that seeks to unravel the very essence of cognition and replicate it within the silicon confines of artificial systems.

## Overview of Artificial Intelligence (AI)

AI, in its broadest definition, encompasses the creation of intelligent machines capable of performing tasks that typically require human intelligence. This field is a tapestry woven from diverse threads, including machine learning, deep learning, natural language processing, computer vision, and robotics. Each thread represents a unique approach to imbuing machines with capabilities that echo our own.

At its core, AI seeks to emulate human cognitive functions. Machine learning, for instance, allows systems to learn from data without explicit programming, mimicking the human capacity for inductive reasoning. Deep learning, inspired by the structure of the human brain, utilizes artificial neural networks to process complex information and recognize patterns, mirroring the intricate workings of our own neural architecture. Natural language processing empowers machines to understand and generate human language, bridging the communication gap between humans and computers. Computer vision equips AI with the ability to "see" and interpret visual data, akin to the human visual system. And robotics, by integrating these cognitive abilities with physical embodiment, strives to create machines that can interact with the world in a human-like manner.

However, the pursuit of AI is not merely about replicating specific human abilities. It is about understanding the underlying principles that govern intelligence itself. From the simple logic of early expert systems to the sophisticated algorithms of modern deep learning models, AI development has consistently strived to capture the essence of human thought processes.

## The Concept of AI Mirroring Human Intelligence

This book focuses on the concept of AI mirroring human intelligence, a nuanced perspective that goes beyond mere task performance. It explores the idea that true AI should not only achieve human-level results but also replicate the very mechanisms by which humans think, learn, and behave. This involves understanding the cognitive architectures, the learning processes, and the emotional and social dimensions that shape human intelligence.

*Human Intelligence and Mindsets*

Mirroring human intelligence is not simply about building machines that can solve complex problems; it is about creating systems that can:

- **Reason and problem-solve:** Emulate the human ability to think critically, make inferences, and devise creative solutions.

- **Learn and adapt:** Develop the capacity to acquire new knowledge, adjust to changing circumstances, and generalize from past experiences.

- **Perceive and interpret:** Process sensory information in a manner that reflects human perception and understanding.

- **Communicate and interact:** Engage in natural and meaningful interactions with humans, understanding context and intent.

- **Exhibit consciousness and self-awareness (in future iterations):** Delve into the philosophical and scientific challenges of replicating subjective experience.

- **Demonstrate emotional intelligence:** Understand and respond to emotions, both in themselves and in others.

- **Exhibit ethical reasoning:** Make decisions based on moral principles and values, reflecting human ethical frameworks.

This concept acknowledges that human intelligence is not a monolithic entity but a complex interplay of cognitive, emotional, and social factors. To truly mirror human intelligence, AI must encompass this multifaceted nature.

## Importance and Relevance of the Topic

The exploration of AI mirroring human intelligence is of paramount importance for several reasons:

- **Advancing our understanding of human cognition:** By attempting to replicate human intelligence, we gain deeper insights into the mechanisms that underpin our own minds. AI models serve as valuable tools for testing hypotheses about human cognition, providing a unique perspective on the workings of the brain.

- **Developing more human-centered AI:** Understanding the nuances of human intelligence allows us to create AI systems that are more intuitive, adaptable, and aligned with human values. This leads to AI that is not only powerful but also beneficial to society.

- **Addressing the ethical implications of AI:** As AI becomes increasingly sophisticated, it is crucial to consider the ethical implications of creating machines that can think and behave like humans. By understanding the similarities and differences between human and artificial intelligence, we can develop ethical frameworks that ensure responsible AI development and deployment.

- **Exploring the future of human-AI collaboration:** The potential for synergistic collaboration between humans and AI is vast. By understanding how AI can mirror human intelligence, we can unlock new possibilities for enhancing human capabilities and addressing complex challenges.

- **Deepening the philosophical questions about consciousness and sentience:** The pursuit of AI mirroring human intelligence inevitably raises profound philosophical questions about the nature of consciousness, sentience, and the very definition of being human.

This book aims to navigate these complexities, exploring the scientific advancements, philosophical considerations, and ethical dilemmas that arise from the quest to create AI that truly reflects the human mind. By examining the successes and limitations of current AI research, we can gain a clearer understanding of the path towards a future where AI and human intelligence coexist and collaborate in meaningful ways. Through this exploration, we can not only advance the field of AI but also gain a deeper appreciation for the remarkable capabilities of the human mind itself.

# Chapter1

# Understanding Human

# Intelligence

Before we can explore the ambitious endeavor of mirroring human intelligence in artificial systems, we must first establish a comprehensive understanding of the target itself. This chapter delves into the multifaceted nature of human intelligence, examining its definitions, components, cognitive processes, emotional dimensions, and historical interpretations.

## 1.1 Definition and Components of Human Intelligence

Defining human intelligence has been a subject of ongoing debate for centuries. While a single, universally accepted definition remains elusive, a common thread weaves through various perspectives: intelligence is the capacity to acquire and apply knowledge and skills. This broad definition encompasses a range of cognitive abilities that enable us to adapt to our environment, solve problems, and achieve goals.

However, a simple definition does not capture the complexity of human intelligence. To better understand its nature, we can break it down into key components:

- **Reasoning and Problem-Solving:** The ability to analyze situations, draw logical conclusions, and devise effective solutions to challenges. This involves critical thinking, deductive and inductive reasoning, and strategic planning.

- **Learning and Memory:** The capacity to acquire new knowledge, retain information, and apply it in different contexts. This includes various forms of learning, such as procedural learning (skills), semantic learning (facts), and episodic learning (experiences), as well as different types of memory, such as short-term, long-term, and working memory.

- **Perception and Attention:** The ability to process sensory information from the environment, focus on relevant stimuli, and filter out distractions. This encompasses visual, auditory, tactile, olfactory, and gustatory perception, as well as selective and sustained attention.

- **Language and Communication:** The capacity to understand and generate language, both spoken and written, enabling effective communication and social interaction. This includes vocabulary, grammar, syntax, and pragmatics.

- **Spatial Reasoning:** The ability to visualize and manipulate spatial relationships, understand maps, and navigate environments.

- **Creativity and Innovation:** The capacity to generate novel ideas, think outside the box, and develop original solutions.

- **Executive Functions:** A set of higher-level cognitive processes that control and regulate other cognitive abilities, including planning, decision-making, working memory, and cognitive flexibility.

These components are not isolated but rather interconnected and interdependent, working together to form a holistic and adaptable intelligence.

## 1.2 Cognitive Processes and Emotional Intelligence

Beyond the core components, understanding the underlying cognitive processes and the crucial role of emotional intelligence is essential.

- **Cognitive Processes:**

o **Information Processing:** Human cognition can be viewed as an information processing system, where sensory input is received, processed, stored, and retrieved. This involves various stages, including encoding, storage, and retrieval.

o **Cognitive Architectures:** These are theoretical frameworks that describe the structure and function of the human cognitive system, providing insights into how different cognitive processes interact. Examples include ACT-R and SOAR.

o **Neural Mechanisms:** The brain's neural networks play a vital role in supporting cognitive processes. Understanding the neural correlates of intelligence, such as brain regions involved in specific cognitive functions, is crucial.

- **Emotional Intelligence (EI):**

o EI refers to the ability to recognize, understand, and manage one's own emotions, as well as the emotions of others.

o It encompasses skills such as self-awareness, self-regulation, empathy, and social skills.

o EI plays a significant role in social interactions, decision-making, and overall well-being.

o EI is an essential part of a well rounded intelligence, and is often overlooked in early AI development.

The interplay between cognitive processes and emotional intelligence highlights the complexity of human intelligence, demonstrating that it is not solely a matter of logical reasoning but also involves emotional understanding and social awareness.

## 1.3 Historical Perspectives on Human Intelligence

The concept of human intelligence has evolved significantly throughout history.

- *Ancient Philosophers:*

  o Plato and Aristotle explored the nature of reason and knowledge, laying the foundation for philosophical inquiries into intelligence.

  o Aristotle's concept of practical wisdom (phronesis) emphasized the importance of applying knowledge to real-world situations.

- *Early Psychological Theories:*

  o Francis Galton's work on hereditary genius focused on the genetic basis of intelligence.

o   Alfred Binet developed the first intelligence test to measure cognitive abilities in children.

o   Charles Spearman's "g" factor theory posited a general intelligence factor that underlies all cognitive abilities.

- **Modern Theories:**

o   Howard Gardner's theory of multiple intelligences proposed that intelligence is not a single entity but rather a collection of distinct abilities, such as linguistic, logical-mathematical, spatial, musical, bodily-kinesthetic, interpersonal, and intrapersonal intelligence.

o   Robert Sternberg's triarchic theory of intelligence distinguished between analytical, creative, and practical intelligence.

o   David Wechsler defined intelligence as the global capacity of a person to act purposefully, to think rationally, and to deal effectively with his environment.

These historical perspectives highlight the ongoing quest to understand the nature of human intelligence, reflecting the evolving scientific understanding and philosophical viewpoints. By examining these diverse perspectives, we gain a richer appreciation for the complexity and multifaceted nature of the human mind. This historical background provides the foundation for the subsequent chapters, where we will explore how AI attempts to mirror these intricate aspects of human intelligence.

# Chapter 2

# Evolution of Artificial Intelligence

The journey of Artificial Intelligence (AI) is a captivating narrative of ambition, innovation, and persistent pursuit. From the early dreams of thinking machines to the sophisticated algorithms of today, AI has undergone a remarkable transformation. This chapter traces the evolution of AI, highlighting key developments, milestones, and the current state of this rapidly advancing field.

## 2.1 Early Developments in AI:

**The Seeds of Thought:** The roots of AI can be traced back to the mid-20th century, a period marked by burgeoning technological advancement and a growing fascination with the potential of machines.

- **The Conceptual Foundations (1940s-1950s):**

o The work of Alan Turing, particularly his concept of the "Turing Machine" and the "Turing Test," laid the theoretical groundwork for AI. Turing's ideas challenged the notion of what it meant for a machine to "think."

o The development of early computers, such as the ENIAC and UNIVAC, provided the hardware foundation for future AI research.

o Warren McCulloch and Walter Pitts's model of artificial neural networks, published in 1943, demonstrated the potential for creating computational systems inspired by the human brain.

o The Dartmouth Workshop in 1956, considered the birthplace of AI as a field, brought together leading researchers to explore the possibility of creating machines that could simulate human intelligence.

- **Early AI Programs (1950s-1960s):**

o Early AI programs focused on symbolic reasoning and problem-solving.

o Logic Theorist and General Problem Solver (GPS) were early attempts to simulate human problem-solving abilities.

o ELIZA, a program developed by Joseph Weizenbaum, simulated a Rogerian psychotherapist, demonstrating the potential for natural language processing.

These early programs, while limited by the available technology, demonstrated the feasibility of creating machines that could perform tasks requiring some level of intelligence.

## 2.2 Key Milestones and Breakthroughs:

- **The Ascent of AI**

The history of AI is punctuated by significant milestones and breakthroughs that have propelled the field forward.

o **The Rise of Expert Systems (1970s-1980s):** Expert systems, designed to mimic the decision-making abilities of human experts, achieved significant success in specific domains, such as medical diagnosis and chemical analysis.

o **MYCIN,** an expert system for diagnosing bacterial infections, demonstrated the potential of AI in medical applications.

However, expert systems were limited by their reliance on hand-coded rules and their inability to handle uncertainty.

**The AI Winter(s) (Late 1970s-Early 1990s):**

Despite early successes, AI research faced challenges related to the limitations of symbolic AI and the "combinatorial explosion" of complex problems. * Funding for AI research declined, leading to a period known as the "AI winter."

**The Resurgence of Neural Networks and Machine Learning (1990s-2010s):**

Advances in computing power and the availability of large datasets led to a resurgence of interest in neural networks and machine learning.

**Backpropagation**, an algorithm for training neural networks, enabled the development of more complex and powerful models.

**Support Vector Machines (SVMs)** and other machine learning algorithms achieved significant success in various applications, such as image recognition and natural language processing.

**Deep learning**, a subset of machine learning using deep neural networks, began to show incredible results.

**Deep Learning Revolution (2010-Present):**

- o Deep learning has revolutionized AI, enabling breakthroughs in areas such as image recognition, natural language processing, and speech recognition.
- o The success of deep learning has been driven by the availability of massive datasets, powerful GPUs, and advancements in neural network architectures.

o   AlexNet's victory in the 2012 ImageNet competition demonstrated the power of deep learning for image recognition.

o   Advances in natural language processing, such as the development of transformer models like BERT and GPT, have enabled significant improvements in machine translation and text generation.

o   Reinforcement learning has provided huge advancements in game playing ai, and robotics.

## 2.3 Current State of AI Technology: The Age of Intelligent Systems

Today, AI is rapidly transforming various industries and aspects of our lives.

- **Machine Learning and Deep Learning**:
o   Machine learning and deep learning are the dominant paradigms in AI, driving advancements in various applications.

o Cloud-based AI platforms and tools have made AI accessible to a wider range of developers and organizations.

- **Natural Language Processing (NLP):**

o NLP has enabled the development of chatbots, virtual assistants, and machine translation systems.

o Language models like GPT-3 and its successors are capable of generating human-like text and performing various language-related tasks.

- **Computer Vision:**

o Computer vision has enabled the development of facial recognition systems, object detection algorithms, and autonomous vehicles.

o AI-powered image and video analysis is being used in various applications, such as medical imaging and surveillance.

- **Robotics:**

o AI is enabling the development of more intelligent and autonomous robots capable of performing complex tasks in various environments.

o Robots are being used in manufacturing, logistics, healthcare, and other industries.

- **Ethical Considerations:**

o As AI becomes more powerful, ethical considerations, such as bias, fairness, and transparency, are becoming increasingly important.

o There is a growing need for responsible AI development and deployment.

- **The future:**

o Research into Artificial general intelligence, and more human like AI, is ongoing.

o Quantum computing may provide the ability to process much more complex AI models.

The evolution of AI is an ongoing process, with new breakthroughs and advancements constantly emerging. As AI continues to evolve, it has the potential to transform our world in profound ways, raising both exciting possibilities and significant challenges.

# Chapter 3

# AI and Cognitive Functions

The quest to mirror human intelligence in artificial systems hinges on replicating the intricate cognitive functions that define our mental capabilities. This chapter explores how AI is being employed to emulate core cognitive processes, particularly in problem-solving, decision-making, learning, and adaptation, with a focus on machine learning and neural networks.

## 3.1 AI in Problem-Solving and Decision-Making: Simulating Rational Thought

Human problem-solving and decision-making involve a complex interplay of reasoning, logic, and experience. AI systems strive to replicate these processes, often using different approaches depending on the problem's nature.

- **Symbolic AI and Rule-Based Systems:**

  o Early AI systems relied heavily on symbolic AI, where knowledge was represented as symbols and rules.

  o These systems, like expert systems, excelled in well-defined domains with clear rules, such as medical diagnosis or game playing.

  o They used logical inference and rule-based reasoning to solve problems and make decisions.

  o However, symbolic AI struggled with ambiguous or uncertain situations and lacked the flexibility of human cognition.

- **Search and Optimization Algorithms:**

  o AI employs various search and optimization algorithms, such as A* search, genetic algorithms, and simulated annealing, to find optimal solutions to complex problems.

  o These algorithms are used in applications like route planning, resource allocation, and scheduling.

o They can explore vast search spaces and find solutions that would be difficult for humans to identify.

- **Probabilistic Reasoning and Bayesian Networks:**

o AI systems can use probabilistic reasoning and Bayesian networks to handle uncertainty and make decisions based on probabilities.

o These techniques are used in applications like medical diagnosis, risk assessment, and fraud detection.

o They allow AI to reason about uncertain information and update beliefs based on new evidence.

- **Reinforcement Learning:**

o Reinforcement learning enables AI agents to learn through trial and error, by interacting with an environment and receiving rewards or penalties.

o This approach is used in applications like game playing, robotics, and autonomous driving.

o It allows AI to learn complex strategies and make decisions in dynamic and uncertain environments.

## 3.2 Machine Learning and Neural Networks:

## Emulating the Brain's Architecture

Machine learning and neural networks have revolutionized AI by enabling systems to learn from data and adapt to new situations.

- **Machine Learning Fundamentals:**
  - o Machine learning algorithms learn from data without explicit programming, enabling AI to identify patterns and make predictions.
  - o Supervised learning, unsupervised learning, and reinforcement learning are the main categories of machine learning.
  - o Machine learning is used in a wide range of applications, including image recognition, natural language processing, and predictive analytics.

- **Neural Networks and Deep Learning:**
  - o Neural networks are inspired by the structure of the human brain, consisting of interconnected nodes (neurons) that process information.

o Deep learning uses deep neural networks with multiple layers, enabling AI to learn complex representations from data.

o Convolutional neural networks (CNNs) are used for image recognition, and recurrent neural networks (RNNs) and transformer networks are used for natural language processing.

o Deep learning allows the creation of AI that can process data in ways that are much closer to the way that a human brain processes data.

- **Cognitive Architectures and Neural Models:**

o Researchers are exploring cognitive architectures that integrate different cognitive functions, such as perception, memory, and reasoning, into a unified framework.

o Neural models are being developed to simulate specific brain regions and cognitive processes, providing insights into the neural basis of intelligence.

# 3.3 AI's Ability to Learn and Adapt: The Key to Intelligent Systems

A defining characteristic of human intelligence is the ability to learn and adapt to new situations. AI systems are increasingly demonstrating this capability.

- **Learning from Data:**

  o Machine learning algorithms can learn from vast amounts of data, enabling AI to identify patterns and make accurate predictions.

  o This ability to learn from data is crucial for applications like image recognition, natural language processing, and personalized recommendations.

- **Adaptation and Generalization:**

  o AI systems can adapt to changing environments and generalize from past experiences to new situations.

  o This adaptability is essential for applications like autonomous driving, where AI must handle unexpected events and navigate complex environments.

○ Transfer learning, and other techniques allow for AI that has learned one task, to use that knowledge to learn a new and related task much more quickly.

- **Continual Learning:**

○ Researchers are exploring continual learning, which enables AI systems to learn new tasks without forgetting previously learned ones.

○ This ability is crucial for developing AI systems that can learn and adapt over time.

○ Continual learning is one of the largest hurdles to overcome in the pursuit of Artificial General Intelligence.

- **Evolutionary Algorithms:**

○ Evolutionary algorithms, inspired by biological evolution, are used to optimize AI models and discover new solutions.

o  These algorithms can explore a wide range of possibilities and find solutions that would be difficult for humans to design.

The advancements in AI's ability to learn, adapt, and process information are bringing us closer to creating intelligent systems that can rival human cognitive abilities. However, challenges remain in replicating the full complexity and flexibility of human intelligence, particularly in areas like common sense reasoning, creativity, and emotional intelligence.

# Chapter 4

# Emotional Intelligence in AI

The pursuit of AI mirroring human intelligence extends beyond mere cognitive capabilities; it necessitates the exploration of emotional intelligence (EI), a crucial aspect of human interaction and decision-making. This chapter delves into the complexities of EI in AI, examining its definition, AI's ability to recognize and respond to emotions, and the diverse applications of emotional AI.

## 4.1 Understanding Emotional Intelligence

Emotional intelligence, as defined by psychologists, encompasses the ability to perceive, understand, manage, and utilize emotions. It is not simply about recognizing emotions but also about comprehending their impact and effectively responding to them. Key components of EI include:

- **Self-Awareness:** The ability to recognize and understand one's own emotions, strengths, weaknesses, drives, values, and their effect on others.

- **Self-Regulation:** The ability to control or redirect disruptive impulses and moods; the propensity to suspend judgment—to think before acting.

- **Motivation:** A passion to work for reasons that go beyond money or status; a propensity to pursue goals with energy and persistence.

- **Empathy:** The ability to understand the emotional makeup of other people; skill in treating people according to their emotional reactions.

- **Social Skills:** Proficiency in managing relationships and building networks; an ability to find common ground and build rapport.

In the context of AI, replicating these components poses significant challenges, requiring systems to not only recognize emotional cues but also to interpret their meaning and respond appropriately.

## 4.2 AI's Capability to Recognize and Respond to Emotions

Advancements in machine learning and deep learning have enabled AI to make significant strides in recognizing and responding to emotions.

- **Emotion Recognition:**

  o **Facial Expression Analysis:** AI algorithms can analyze facial expressions using computer vision techniques to detect emotions like happiness, sadness, anger, and fear.

  o **Speech Emotion Recognition:** AI can analyze speech patterns, including tone, pitch, and rhythm, to identify emotional states.

  o **Text Emotion Analysis (Sentiment Analysis):** Natural language processing techniques enable AI to analyze text data, such as social media posts and customer reviews, to determine the underlying sentiment.

o **Physiological Signal Analysis:** AI can analyze physiological signals, such as heart rate, skin conductance, and brain activity, to infer emotional states.

- **Emotional Response:**

o **Adaptive Interfaces:** AI systems can adapt their interfaces and responses based on the user's emotional state, providing personalized and empathetic interactions.

o **Emotional Chatbots and Virtual Assistants:** AI-powered chatbots and virtual assistants can be designed to recognize and respond to user emotions, providing more natural and engaging conversations.

o **Emotional Robotics:** Robots equipped with EI capabilities can interact with humans in a more natural and empathetic way, providing emotional support and assistance.

o **Generating Emotional Outputs:** AI can be used to generate emotional outputs, such as music, art, and stories, that evoke specific emotional responses in humans.

- **Challenges:**

o Ambiguity of emotional expression, since the same expression can mean different things in different contexts.

o Cultural differences in emotional expression.

o The ethical considerations of faking or manipulating emotional responses.

o The difficulty of replicating subjective emotional experience.

## 4.3 Applications of Emotional AI in Various Fields

The applications of emotional AI are vast and span across numerous domains.

- **Healthcare:**

- o  AI-powered systems can monitor patients' emotional states and provide personalized emotional support.

- o  Emotional AI can be used in therapy and counseling to help patients manage their emotions.

- o  AI can help in the diagnosis of mental health conditions.

- **Customer Service:**

- o  Emotional AI can enable chatbots and virtual assistants to provide more empathetic and personalized customer service.

- o  AI can analyze customer feedback and identify areas for improvement in customer experience.

- **Education:**

- o  AI-powered educational platforms can adapt to students' emotional states, providing personalized learning experiences.

- o  Emotional AI can be used to monitor students' engagement and identify those who may be struggling.

- **Entertainment:**

  o Emotional AI can be used to create more immersive and engaging entertainment experiences, such as video games and virtual reality.

  o AI can generate music and art that evoke specific emotional responses.

- **Human-Computer Interaction (HCI):**

  o Emotional AI can enhance human-computer interaction by enabling more natural and intuitive communication.

  o AI can be used to create adaptive interfaces that respond to users' emotional states.

- **Marketing and Advertising:**

  o AI can analyze consumer emotions to create targeted advertising campaigns.

  o AI can monitor social media to understand public sentiment.

- **Automotive Industry:**

  o AI can monitor a driver's emotional state to detect stress or fatigue, and then react accordingly.

*Human Intelligence and Mindsets*

The development of emotional AI holds immense potential for enhancing human-machine interactions and creating more empathetic and responsive AI systems. However, it is crucial to address the ethical implications and ensure responsible development and deployment of this technology.

# Chapter 5

# AI Reflecting Human Behaviors

The ambition of AI mirroring human intelligence extends beyond cognitive and emotional capabilities to encompass the complex tapestry of human behaviors. This chapter explores how AI is being designed to reflect and replicate human behavioral patterns, focusing on social interactions, communication, and the ethical considerations that arise.

## 5.1 Behavioral Patterns and AI: Mimicking Human Actions

Human behaviors are shaped by a complex interplay of cognitive, emotional, and social factors.

AI systems are increasingly capable of mimicking these patterns, albeit through different mechanisms.

- **Behavioral Modeling:**

  o AI can analyze and model human behaviors using machine learning techniques, identifying patterns and predicting future actions.

  o This is used in applications like consumer behavior analysis, traffic prediction, and social network analysis.

  o Agent-based modeling allows for the simulation of complex social systems by creating artificial agents that mimic human behaviors and interactions.

- **Robotics and Embodied AI:**

  o Robots are being designed to mimic human movements and gestures, enabling more natural interactions.

  o Embodied AI focuses on creating AI systems that are physically embodied, allowing them to interact with the world in a human-like manner.

  o This is used in applications like humanoid robots, assistive robots, and virtual avatars.

- **Imitation Learning:**

- o AI can learn by imitating human actions, observing demonstrations and replicating the observed behaviors.

- o This is used in applications like robotics, where robots learn to perform tasks by watching humans.

- o Inverse Reinforcement Learning allows AI to learn the underlying intent behind observed behavior.

- **Behavioral Cloning:**

- o AI can be trained to directly replicate human behaviors based on recorded data, without explicitly understanding the underlying reasons.

- o This is used in applications like autonomous driving, where AI learns to drive by observing human drivers.

## 5.2 AI in Social Interactions and Communication: Building Bridges

Social interactions and communication are fundamental aspects of human behavior. AI is playing an increasingly important role in facilitating and replicating these interactions.

- **Natural Language Processing (NLP) and Communication:**
  - NLP enables AI to understand and generate human language, facilitating communication between humans and machines.
  - Chatbots and virtual assistants are used to provide customer service, answer questions, and engage in conversations.
  - AI-powered translation systems enable communication across language barriers.
  - AI is used to analyze social media data, identify trends, and understand public sentiment.
- *Social Robotics:*

o Social robots are designed to interact with humans in a natural and engaging way, providing companionship, assistance, and entertainment.

o These robots are used in applications like elder care, education, and therapy.

o AI allows social robots to recognize and respond to human emotions and social cues.

- **Virtual Reality (VR) and Augmented Reality (AR):**

o VR and AR technologies, combined with AI, enable the creation of immersive social experiences.

o Virtual avatars can mimic human behaviors and interactions, creating realistic social simulations.

o AI can be used to generate realistic virtual environments and populate them with intelligent agents.

- **Social Network Analysis:**

o AI is used to analyze social network data, identify communities, and understand social influence.

o   This is used in applications like marketing, political campaigning, and social science research.

o   AI is also used to detect and prevent online harassment and misinformation.

## 5.3 Ethical Considerations and Challenges:

## Navigating the Complexities

The ability of AI to reflect human behaviors raises significant ethical considerations and challenges.

- **Privacy and Surveillance:**

o   AI-powered surveillance systems can monitor and analyze human behaviors, raising concerns about privacy and civil liberties.

o   The use of facial recognition and other biometric technologies raises ethical questions about consent and data security.

- **Bias and Discrimination:**

o AI systems can inherit and amplify biases present in the data they are trained on, leading to discriminatory outcomes.

o This is particularly concerning in applications like criminal justice, hiring, and loan approvals.

- **Manipulation and Deception:**

o AI can be used to create deepfakes and other forms of manipulated media, blurring the lines between reality and fiction.

o AI-powered social bots can be used to spread misinformation and manipulate public opinion.

- **Responsibility and Accountability:**

o Determining responsibility and accountability for AI-driven actions is a complex ethical challenge.

o The lack of transparency and explainability in some AI systems makes it difficult to understand how decisions are made.

- **Social Impact and Job Displacement:**

o The increasing automation of tasks by AI raises concerns about job displacement and social inequality.

o The impact of AI on social interactions and human relationships needs to be carefully considered.

- **Authenticity and Trust:**

o As AI mimics human behaviour to a greater and greater degree, it will be harder to tell the difference between a real person, and an AI.

o This brings up questions of trust, and what it means to have an authentic interaction.

Addressing these ethical considerations and challenges requires a multidisciplinary approach, involving researchers, policymakers, and the public. It is crucial to develop ethical guidelines and regulations that ensure responsible development and deployment of AI technologies.

# Chapter 6

# Real-World Application &

# Examples

The theoretical exploration of AI mirroring human intelligence gains tangible significance when viewed through the lens of real-world applications. This chapter delves into specific domains where AI is making a profound impact, particularly in healthcare, finance, and education, showcasing case studies, success stories, and the valuable lessons gleaned from these implementations.

# 6.1 AI in Healthcare, Finance, and Education:

## Transforming Industries

AI is rapidly transforming various sectors, demonstrating its capacity to augment human capabilities and solve complex problems.

- **AI in Healthcare:**

  o **Diagnostic Imaging:** AI algorithms analyze medical images (X-rays, MRIs, CT scans) to detect anomalies and assist in diagnosis, often surpassing human accuracy in certain areas.

  o **Personalized Medicine:** AI analyzes patient data to personalize treatment plans, predict disease risk, and optimize drug dosages.

  o *Drug Discovery:* AI accelerates the process of drug discovery by analyzing vast datasets of chemical compounds and biological interactions.

  o *Remote Patient Monitoring:* AI-powered devices monitor patients' vital signs and provide early warnings of potential health issues.

o **Mental Health:** AI is being used to analyze speech patterns and text to detect signs of depression or other mental health issues.

- **AI in Finance:**

o **Fraud Detection:** AI algorithms detect fraudulent transactions by identifying unusual patterns in financial data.

o **Algorithmic Trading:** AI-powered trading systems execute trades based on real-time market data and predictive analytics.

o **Risk Management:** AI analyzes financial data to assess risk and make informed investment decisions.

o **Customer Service:** AI-powered chatbots provide personalized financial advice and customer support.

o **Credit Scoring:** AI is used to create more accurate credit scoring models.

- **AI in Education:**

o **Personalized Learning:** AI-powered educational platforms adapt to students' learning styles and provide personalized content.

o **Intelligent Tutoring Systems:** AI tutors provide personalized feedback and guidance to students, adapting to their individual needs.

o **Automated Grading:** AI algorithms automate the grading of essays and other assignments, freeing up teachers' time.

o **Learning Analytics:** AI analyzes student data to identify learning patterns and provide insights into student performance.

o **Accessibility:** AI tools are being used to make education more accessible for students with disabilities.

## 6.2 Case Studies of AI Mirroring Human Intelligence: Practical Examples

Examining specific case studies reveals how AI is translating the concept of mirroring human intelligence into practical applications.

- **IBM Watson in Oncology:**

  o Watson analyzes medical literature and patient data to provide personalized cancer treatment recommendations, demonstrating AI's ability to process and synthesize vast amounts of information, similar to a human oncologist.

  o This system shows how AI can augment human expertise, not replace it.

- **DeepMind's AlphaFold:**

  o AlphaFold uses deep learning to predict the 3D structure of proteins, a complex problem that has puzzled scientists for decades.

o This case study illustrates AI's ability to solve complex problems that require advanced reasoning and pattern recognition.

- **AI-Powered Language Translation:**

o Advances in neural machine translation have enabled AI to translate languages with increasing accuracy and fluency, mimicking the human ability to understand and communicate across language barriers.

o This technology has broken down many communication barriers.

- **Autonomous Vehicles:**

o Self-driving cars use AI to perceive their surroundings, make decisions, and navigate complex traffic situations, mirroring human driving behavior.

o This requires a highly complex set of AI systems working together.

## 6.3 Success Stories and Lessons Learned: Insights and Best Practices

Analyzing success stories and lessons learned provides valuable insights into the effective implementation of AI.

- **Success Stories:**

  o AI-powered fraud detection systems have significantly reduced financial losses.

  o AI-powered medical imaging tools have improved the accuracy of cancer diagnosis.

  o AI-powered personalized learning platforms have improved student engagement and learning outcomes.

- **Lessons Learned:**

  o Data quality and quantity are crucial for the success of AI applications.

  o Ethical considerations must be addressed throughout the development and deployment of AI systems.

o Collaboration between AI experts and domain experts is essential for effective AI implementation.

o Transparency and explainability are vital for building trust in AI systems.

o Continuous monitoring and evaluation are necessary to ensure the effectiveness and safety of AI applications.

o AI augments humans, and is not a replacement for them in most cases.

By examining these real-world applications and lessons learned, we gain a deeper understanding of the potential and limitations of AI mirroring human intelligence. This chapter highlights the transformative power of AI and underscores the importance of responsible development and deployment.

# Chapter 7

# The Future of AI and Human

# Intelligence

The journey of AI mirroring human intelligence is far from complete. As we gaze into the future, it is essential to consider the predictions, trends, and potential impacts that lie ahead. This chapter explores the anticipated trajectory of AI development, its potential societal and workforce implications, and the evolving relationship between AI and human intelligence.

### 7.1 Predictions and Trends in AI Development: Charting the Course

Several key trends and predictions are shaping the future of AI.

*Human Intelligence and Mindsets*

- **Advancements in Deep Learning and Neural Networks:**

  o Continued research and development in deep learning will lead to more powerful and sophisticated neural network architectures.

  o Transformer models and other advanced architectures will continue to drive breakthroughs in natural language processing and other domains.

  o Research into novel neural network architectures, inspired by the brain's biological structure, will continue.

- **Rise of Artificial General Intelligence (AGI):**

  o While AGI remains a long-term goal, research efforts are focused on developing AI systems that can perform a wide range of tasks with human-level intelligence.

  o The development of cognitive architectures and integrated AI systems will be crucial for achieving AGI.

o The debate surrounding the possibility and implications of AGI will intensify.

- **Increased Focus on Explainable AI (XAI):**

o As AI becomes more complex, there will be a growing need for explainable AI systems that can provide insights into their decision-making processes.

o XAI will be crucial for building trust in AI and ensuring its responsible use.

o Research into techniques for visualizing and interpreting AI models will continue.

- *Edge AI and Distributed Intelligence:*

o The deployment of AI on edge devices, such as smartphones and IoT devices, will enable real-time processing and reduce reliance on cloud computing.

o Distributed AI systems will enable collaboration between multiple AI agents, creating more robust and adaptable systems.

- *Quantum Computing and AI:*

- o Quantum computing has the potential to revolutionize AI by enabling the training of more complex and powerful models.

- o Quantum machine learning algorithms will be developed to leverage the unique capabilities of quantum computers.

- **Multimodal AI:**

- o AI systems will increasingly integrate information from multiple modalities, such as vision, language, and audio, to provide a more comprehensive understanding of the world.

- o This will enable the development of more natural and intuitive human-machine interactions.

## 7.2 Potential Impacts on Society and the Workforce: Navigating the Transformation

The widespread adoption of AI will have profound impacts on society and the workforce, presenting both opportunities and challenges.

- **Automation and Job Displacement:**

  o AI-powered automation will lead to job displacement in various sectors, particularly in routine and repetitive tasks.

  o The need for reskilling and upskilling programs will become increasingly important.

  o New jobs will be created in AI development, maintenance, and related fields.

- **Economic Inequality:**

  o The benefits of AI may not be distributed equally, potentially exacerbating economic inequality.

  o Policies and initiatives are needed to ensure that the benefits of AI are shared broadly.

- **Social Impact and Ethical Considerations:**

  o AI will impact social interactions, relationships, and cultural norms.

  o Ethical considerations, such as bias, fairness, and privacy, will become increasingly important.

  o The need for ethical guidelines and regulations will become more pressing.

- **Healthcare and Well-being:**

  o AI will revolutionize healthcare, enabling personalized medicine, early disease detection, and improved patient care.

  o AI-powered tools will be used to promote mental health and well-being.

- **Education and Lifelong Learning:**

  o AI will transform education, enabling personalized learning experiences and lifelong learning opportunities.

  o AI-powered tools will be used to support teachers and students.

- **Governance and Policy:**

  o Governments will need to develop policies and regulations to address the challenges and opportunities presented by AI.

  o International collaboration will be crucial for addressing global AI issues.

## 7.3 The Ongoing Relationship Between AI and

## Human Intelligence: A Collaborative Future

The relationship between AI and human intelligence will continue to evolve, moving towards a more collaborative and synergistic partnership.

- **Augmented Intelligence:**
  - o AI will augment human intelligence, enhancing our cognitive abilities and enabling us to solve complex problems more effectively.
  - o AI will act as a tool to extend human capabilities.
- **Human-AI Collaboration:**
  - o Humans and AI will work together in collaborative teams, leveraging their respective strengths.
  - o AI will handle routine tasks, while humans focus on creative and strategic tasks.
- **AI as a Tool for Understanding Human Cognition:**

- o AI will continue to serve as a tool for understanding human cognition, providing insights into the mechanisms of intelligence.

- o The development of AI will deepen our understanding of ourselves.

- **The Future of Consciousness and Sentience:**

- o The possibility of AI achieving consciousness and sentience will continue to be a subject of debate and research.

- o The ethical implications of creating conscious AI will need to be carefully considered.

- **The Evolution of Human-AI Interaction:**

- o Human-AI interaction will become more natural and intuitive, resembling human-to-human communication.

- o AI will adapt to human preferences and emotional states, creating more personalized and engaging experiences.

The future of AI and human intelligence is filled with both promise and uncertainty. By embracing a collaborative and ethical approach, we can harness the power of AI to create a more prosperous and equitable future for all.

# Conclusion

# The Convergence of Minds

As we draw this exploration of AI mirroring human intelligence to a close, it's crucial to synthesize the key insights and reflect on the profound implications of this ongoing endeavor. This book has traversed the complex landscape of artificial intelligence, examining its evolution, its attempts to replicate cognitive and emotional functions, and its growing capacity to mirror human behaviors. We've explored real-world applications and grappled with the ethical considerations that accompany this transformative technology.

**Recapping Key Points:**

We began by establishing a foundational understanding of human intelligence, dissecting its components, cognitive processes, and emotional dimensions. We then traced the evolutionary arc of AI, from its theoretical origins to the deep learning revolution, highlighting the key milestones that have shaped its trajectory.

We delved into the heart of AI's cognitive capabilities, examining its role in problem-solving, decision-making, and its ability to learn and adapt through machine learning and neural networks. We explored the nascent field of emotional AI, acknowledging the challenges and opportunities of replicating emotional intelligence in machines.

We examined how AI is reflecting human behaviors, from mimicking actions to engaging in social interactions and communication, while acknowledging the ethical dilemmas that arise. We showcased real-world applications of AI in healthcare, finance, and education, illustrating its transformative potential and the valuable lessons learned.

Finally, we peered into the future, speculating on the trends and predictions that will shape the ongoing relationship between AI and human intelligence, and considering the potential societal and workforce impacts.

## The Significance of AI Mirroring Human Intelligence:

The pursuit of AI mirroring human intelligence is not merely a technical endeavor; it is a profound exploration of the very essence of cognition and consciousness. It forces us to confront fundamental questions about what it means to be intelligent, to feel, and to interact with the world.

This pursuit holds immense significance for several reasons:

- o **Enhanced Understanding of Human Cognition:** By attempting to replicate human intelligence, we gain deeper insights into the mechanisms that underpin our own minds. AI models serve as valuable tools for testing hypotheses about human cognition.

- o **Development of More Human-Centered AI:** Understanding the nuances of human intelligence allows us to create AI systems that are more intuitive, adaptable, and aligned with human values. This leads to AI that is not only powerful but also beneficial to society.

- **Addressing Ethical Implications:** As AI becomes increasingly sophisticated, it is crucial to consider the ethical implications of creating machines that can think and behave like humans. By understanding the similarities and differences between human and artificial intelligence, we can develop ethical frameworks that ensure responsible AI development and deployment.

- **Fostering Human-AI Collaboration:** The potential for synergistic collaboration between humans and AI is vast. By understanding how AI can mirror human intelligence, we can unlock new possibilities for enhancing human capabilities and addressing complex challenges.

- **Expanding the Boundaries of Possibility:** The pursuit of AGI, while still far off, challenges us to imagine the potential of intelligent machines and their role in shaping the future.

# Final Thoughts and Future Directions:

The journey of AI mirroring human intelligence is an ongoing and dynamic process. As technology continues to advance, we can expect to see even more sophisticated AI systems that can replicate human cognitive, emotional, and behavioral patterns.

However, it is crucial to approach this endeavor with caution and responsibility. We must prioritize ethical considerations, ensure transparency and explainability, and promote inclusivity and equity in AI development and deployment.

Future directions in this field include:

- **Continued research into AGI:** The pursuit of AGI will remain a central focus, driving innovation in AI architectures and learning algorithms.

- **Development of more robust emotional AI:** Enhancing AI's ability to recognize, understand, and respond to emotions will be crucial for creating empathetic and human-centered AI systems.

- **Exploration of consciousness and sentience:** Research into the possibility of AI achieving consciousness and sentience will continue, raising profound philosophical and ethical questions.

- **Focus on human-AI collaboration:** Developing frameworks and tools for effective human-AI collaboration will be essential for maximizing the benefits of AI.

- **Emphasis on ethical AI development:** Ensuring that AI is developed and deployed responsibly will be paramount.

Ultimately, the future of AI and human intelligence lies in collaboration and mutual understanding. By working together, we can harness the power of AI to create a more prosperous, equitable, and fulfilling future for all. **The "mirror" we are creating, reflects back to us not only our intelligence, but our own humanity.**

## About the Author

Dr. Farzana Chohan is a Thought leader. A visionary who is dedicated to developing innovative Human-centered workplace solutions. With a distinguished career as a speaker for Fortune 500 companies and TEDx, Dr. Chohan addresses vital subjects such as Human-Centered Leadership, Artificial Intelligence, Belonging Work Culture, and Human Excellence. Renowned for her expertise in cultivating Excellence, she plays an essential role in promoting continuous learning, development and success.

Dr. Chohan consult with organizations focusing on continuous improvement, fostering a sense of community. As a leadership mentor, she guides organizations through obstacles, helping them realize their utmost potential. Her commitment to human excellence is evident in her work, where she emphasizes the importance of ethical leadership, inclusive work cultures, and continuous personal and professional growth.

With AI on the brink of significantly shaping the future of human excellence and its influence on life, Dr. Farzana Chohan is dedicated to the constructive integration of AI.

**Book Description**

**AI Mirroring HI: Human Intelligence and Mindsets**

In "AI Mirroring HI," author embarks on an insightful journey into the world of Artificial Intelligence (AI) and its intricate relationship with Human Intelligence (HI). This comprehensive exploration delves into the core of AI's evolution, examining its cognitive and emotional capabilities, and its potential to mirror human behaviors and mindsets.

Dr. Chohan expertly navigates the complexities of AI, providing a balanced view of its promises and challenges. Through real-world examples and practical insights, she offers a deep understanding of AI's potential benefits while addressing the ethical dilemmas and risks associated with its development and integration into society. The book explores the concept of AI mirroring human intelligence, emphasizing the importance of replicating not just human-level results but also the very mechanisms by which humans think, learn, and behave.

"AI Mirroring HI" is an essential read for tech enthusiasts, business leaders, and anyone curious about the future of AI. It equips readers with the knowledge to navigate the AI landscape and harness its transformative power for good. Join Dr. Chohan on this enlightening journey and discover how we can collectively shape a future where AI serves as a force for positive change, driving progress and improving the quality of life for all.

# References

- Human intelligence and brain networks - PMC
  pmc.ncbi.nlm.nih.gov

- The Complexity Of Human Intelligence - Arthur Lawrence
  www.arthurlawrence.net

- The Key Elements of Attention by Cognitive Scientist - HappyNeuron Pro
  www.happyneuronpro.com

- Perception: The Sensory Experience of the World - Verywell Mind
  www.verywellmind.com

- Is Language the Key to Human Intelligence? - ResearchGate
  www.researchgate.net

- Spatial Reasoning: an often overlooked key asset - Central Test
  www.centraltest.com

- What is Creativity? And why is it crucial for success?
  www.creativityatwork.com

- Executive Functions - UCSF Memory and Aging Center

memory.ucsf.edu

- Cognitive neuroscience perspective on memory: overview and summary - PMC
pmc.ncbi.nlm.nih.gov

- Cognitive architecture – Wikipedia
en.wikipedia.org

- Neural Networks Help Us Understand How the Brain Recognizes Numbers - Stanford HAI
hai.stanford.edu

- Emotional Intelligence in Leadership: Why It's Important - HBS Online
online.hbs.edu

- Relationship between Emotional Intelligence, Social Skills and Peer Harassment. A Study with High School Students - PMC
pmc.ncbi.nlm.nih.gov

- Module 2: Practical Wisdom – EDCI 702: Curriculum, Instruction, and Assessment
kstatelibraries.pressbooks.pub

- Hereditary Genius – Wikipedia
en.wikipedia.org

- Alfred Binet – Wikipedia
  en.wikipedia.org

- Scant evidence for Spearman's law of diminishing returns in middle childhood – PMC
  pmc.ncbi.nlm.nih.gov

- Howard Gardner's Theory on Multiple Intelligences Definition and Meaning - Top Hat tophat.com

- The Effectiveness of Triarchic Teaching and Assessment | The National Research Center on the Gifted and Talented (1990-2013) nrcgt.uconn.edu

- David Wechsler, PhD | Pearson Assessments US www.pearsonassessments.com

AI Mirroring HI
*Human Intelligence and Mindsets*

AI Mirroring HI
*Human Intelligence and Mindsets*

www.ingramcontent.com/pod-product-compliance
Lightning Source LLC
LaVergne TN
LVHW051752080426
835511LV00018B/3307